# SUMMARY OF THE POWER OF VISION

*Charting Your Spiritual Course*

## MARK COWART

Copyright 2024–Harrison House

All rights reserved. This book is protected by the copyright laws of the United States of America. This book may not be copied or reprinted for commercial gain or profit. The use of short quotations or occasional page copying for personal or group study is permitted and encouraged. Permission will be granted upon request. Unless otherwise indicated, all scripture quotations are taken from the *King James Version* of the Bible. Used by permission. All rights reserved.

All emphasis within Scripture quotations is the author's own. Please note that Harrison House's publishing style capitalizes certain pronouns in Scripture that refer to the Father, Son, and Holy Spirit, and may differ from some publishers' styles. Take note that the name satan and related names are not capitalized. We choose not to acknowledge him, even to the point of violating grammatical rules.

Harrison House P.O. Box 310, Shippensburg, PA 17257-0310

This book and all other Harrison House's books are available at Christian bookstores and distributors worldwide.

For Worldwide Distribution.

Reach us on the Internet: www.harrisonhouse.com.

ISBN 13 TP: 9781667510378

ISBN 13 eBook: 9781667510385

# CONTENTS

| | |
|---|---:|
| Introduction | v |
| 1. Logos vs. Rhema | 1 |
| 2. What Is Vision? | 5 |
| 3. Aligning Your Vision with the Times | 9 |
| 4. Heavenly Vision that Confronts the Gates of Hell | 13 |
| 5. The Power of Right Thinking | 17 |
| 6. The Role of Testing in the Power of Vision | 21 |
| 7. Kingdom Disciples Running with the Heavenly Vision | 25 |
| 8. America: A Modern-Day Manifestation of the Heavenly Vision | 29 |
| About the Publisher | 33 |

# INTRODUCTION

❧

Vision shapes our perception of the world and influences our actions, decisions, and interactions. In the realm of personal development and spiritual growth, the power of vision stands as a fundamental force, driving individuals and communities toward achieving seemingly impossible goals. This book, "The Power of Vision," delves into the profound impact that a clear, purpose-driven vision can have on an individual's life, empowering them to transcend ordinary boundaries and embrace a future filled with potential and promise.

The essence of vision is not merely about setting goals or dreaming big; it's about aligning these aspirations with divine purpose and personal conviction. A true vision is a vivid mental image of what you want your life to be at some point in the future, based on your goals and aspirations. It's a picture so clear and strong it helps make that future a reality. Thus, vision acts as a bridge between present reality and future possibilities.

INTRODUCTION

Throughout this book, we explore various dimensions of vision, from its biblical foundations and spiritual significance to practical steps for cultivating and sustaining it in everyday life. Each chapter is designed to equip you with the knowledge and tools necessary to harness the power of vision, enabling you to see beyond the immediate, navigate challenges with resilience, and create a legacy of lasting impact.

Moreover, this book underscores the importance of a spiritually anchored vision. It illustrates how visions rooted in divine guidance not only lead to personal fulfillment but also contribute to broader societal and spiritual renewal. By weaving together theological insights, historical examples, and contemporary testimonies, "The Power of Vision" provides a comprehensive look at how vision shapes our identity, drives our purpose, and influences our destiny.

As we embark on this journey through the pages of "The Power of Vision," prepare to be inspired, challenged, and transformed. Whether you are seeking direction for personal growth, leadership development, or spiritual depth, this book offers valuable perspectives that will empower you to unlock your potential and pursue a life of significance and purpose.

# CHAPTER 1
# LOGOS VS. RHEMA

**Bible Verse**

"For the word of God is alive and active. Sharper than any double-edged sword, it penetrates even to dividing soul and spirit, joints and marrow; it judges the thoughts and attitudes of the heart." - Hebrews 4:12 (NIV)

**Introduction**

In this enlightening chapter, the author delves into the profound journey of understanding and experiencing the transformative power of God's word through the concepts of *logos* (the written Word) and *rhema* (the spoken or revealed Word). It is a personal exploration rooted in the necessity of grasping these concepts for effective ministry and personal breakthrough.

**Word of Wisdom**

*"Don't be a generational thief! Don't take what it took you a lifetime to learn to*

*the grave with you. Share it with others."*
*Mark Cowart*

## Main Theme

The main theme of this chapter is the distinction between the *logos* and *rhema* and how understanding this difference is crucial for spiritual growth and effectiveness in ministry. The author uses personal experiences and biblical insights to demonstrate how the Word of God can transition from being text on a page to a life-changing revelation.

## Key Points

- The *logos* is the written Word of God, foundational and eternal, as described in John 1:1-4.
- *Rhema* refers to the moment the Holy Spirit activates the Scriptures in us, transforming them into a personal word that impacts our lives directly.
- True spiritual authority and power in Christian life arise when the *logos* becomes *rhema*.
- The transition from *logos* to *rhema* is essential for overcoming spiritual challenges and engaging effectively in spiritual warfare.
- Sharing the insights and revelations from God's word is crucial; it prevents the loss of valuable spiritual wisdom.
- Understanding and applying the *logos* and *rhema* can lead to significant breakthroughs

in personal and communal spiritual endeavors.

## Key Themes

- **The Power of the Word in Personal Growth**: The journey from *logos* to *rhema* is not just about knowledge but about allowing the Word to become alive and active within us. This transformation is necessary for personal spiritual growth and for exercising true faith and authority as believers.
- **Spiritual Warfare and the Word**: In spiritual battles, victory often depends on the *rhema* — the specifically revealed word of God for a situation. This concept is illustrated through the author's encounter with demonic forces, which he overcame by the timely application of *rhema*.
- **Ministry and the Word**: Effective ministry relies on a deep, personal engagement with the Scriptures, moving beyond mere reading to a profound revelation that can be shared with others. This approach not only enriches the individual but also empowers the broader Christian community.
- **The Lifelong Learning of the Word**: The author emphasizes that understanding the Word of God is a lifelong journey. Even after decades in ministry, there is always deeper insight to gain and more to apply in life and service to others.

- **Imparting Wisdom Across Generations**: Highlighting the responsibility to pass on what one has learned, the author challenges readers not to hoard spiritual knowledge but to actively disseminate it, ensuring that valuable lessons are not lost but instead bless others.

## Conclusion

"Logos vs. Rhema" serves as a powerful reminder of the dynamic and living nature of God's Word. The chapter calls believers to engage deeply with Scripture, encouraging them to seek the transformation of the written Word into a personally revealed Word that empowers, enlightens, and enacts God's will in their lives and in the world around them.

## CHAPTER 2

## WHAT IS VISION?

### Bible Verse

"Where there is no vision, the people perish: but he that keepeth the law, happy is he." - Proverbs 29:18 KJV

### Introduction

This chapter explores the concept of vision, emphasizing the critical distinction between natural vision and spiritual vision, the latter being an essential aspect of a believer's life as imparted through biblical teachings. It draws from scriptural narratives and personal insights to underscore the importance of spiritual sight in perceiving and manifesting God's promises.

### Word of Wisdom

*"The enemy would rather have blinded minds than blinded eyes, and the Lord*

*doesn't want either of these things for our lives." Mark Cowart*

## Main Theme

The main theme revolves around the transformative power of spiritual vision which enables believers to see beyond the physical and grasp the eternal realities and promises of God, thereby living out a faith-filled life marked by divine guidance and protection.

## Key Points

- Vision is more than the ability to see physically; it involves understanding and perceiving future possibilities with spiritual insight.
- Spiritual vision is a gift from God, allowing believers to see the realities of the spiritual realm.
- Having spiritual vision is akin to seeing with a second set of eyes, which perceive beyond the natural to the supernatural.
- Elisha's prayer for his servant to see the heavenly host illustrates the power and necessity of spiritual vision.
- Spiritual blindness keeps people in bondage, while spiritual sight leads to freedom and the fulfillment of God's promises.
- The new covenant through Christ enhances our capacity for spiritual vision, equipping us with better promises.

## Key Themes

- **The Dual Nature of Vision**: Vision in the biblical context encompasses both the physical ability to see and a deeper, spiritual foresight enabled by faith. This spiritual vision is crucial for believers to navigate and triumph in their spiritual journey.
- **Historical and Scriptural Precedents**: The concept of spiritual sight is backed by numerous biblical examples, such as Elisha's servant seeing the armies of God, which illustrates how spiritual realities can empower and protect believers.
- **Impact of Spiritual Blindness vs. Spiritual Sight**: Spiritual blindness is depicted as a debilitating state that can lead believers into bondage, whereas spiritual sight offers liberation and access to God's immense provisions and promises.
- **The Role of Light in Vision**: Just as natural sight requires light to function effectively, spiritual vision needs the 'light' of God's word to discern and understand the spiritual truths and divine directions intended for us.
- **Renewal and Transformation through Vision**: Embracing spiritual vision leads to a transformative renewal of the mind, enabling believers to align more closely with God's purposes and experience a life of victory and fulfillment.

## Conclusion

Understanding and cultivating spiritual vision is not just an optional aspect of Christian faith, but a vital necessity that enables believers to perceive, engage with, and manifest the realities of God's kingdom. This vision empowers them to live out their divine purpose and bring light to those in darkness. Through spiritual sight, we access the fullness of life Christ offers, making it imperative for every believer to seek this vision through the word and prayer.

CHAPTER 3

# ALIGNING YOUR VISION WITH THE TIMES

### Bible Verse

"Unveil thou mine eyes, and I shall perceive wondrous things of thy law." - Psalm 119:18, Brenton Septuagint Translation

### Introduction

This chapter underscores the crucial role of having a God-inspired vision in a turbulent world. It illustrates the importance of aligning personal and collective visions with God's timing to bring about faith, hope, and deliverance in times of global distress.

### Word of Wisdom

*"Remember that you or your organization must give life to the mission through the dynamics of vision, commitment, and energy, which provide the fuel that will give it life." Mark Cowart*

## Main Theme

The main theme is the transformative power of a clear, God-given vision, especially in challenging times. It highlights the necessity of writing down one's vision to ensure clarity and commitment, as well as the importance of timing in realizing these visions.

## Key Points

- A God-sized vision is essential in today's world to counteract despair and bring deliverance.
- Spiritual blindness limits potential, while spiritual vision opens the way to God's power.
- Writing down the vision is a biblical principle that helps in remembering and focusing efforts.
- The right timing, or seizing God-appointed opportunities, is crucial for the fulfillment of any vision.
- Vision must align with God's broader purposes and requires personal and collective commitment to actualize.
- The realization of vision involves a partnership between divine guidance and human action.

## Key Themes

- **The Necessity of Spiritual Vision**: Just as physical sight is crucial for navigating the physical world, spiritual vision is indispensable for understanding and engaging effectively with spiritual realities. It allows believers to see beyond the immediate and perceive God's larger plan.

- **The Role of Written Vision**: Documenting one's vision as inspired by God ensures it is not forgotten and helps maintain focus on the goals set. It acts as a reminder of one's duties and responsibilities, which is especially important when facing challenges or distractions.
- **The Importance of Timing in Vision**: God's timing is perfect, and aligning one's efforts with this divine schedule is crucial for the successful realization of visions. Understanding and waiting for the right time underpins many biblical stories of success and is a key factor in contemporary spiritual endeavors.
- **Integrating Vision with Action**: Vision without action is ineffective. This theme emphasizes the believer's role as a co-laborer with God, where God provides the spiritual insight and believers must act to bring the vision to fruition.
- **The Impact of Vision on the Community**: A well-articulated and timely vision has the power to transform not just individual lives but entire communities. By shining God's light through their actions, believers can guide many out of spiritual darkness into hope and salvation.

## Conclusion

"Aligning Your Vision with the Times" calls for a proactive stance in understanding and fulfilling God's purpose through well-defined, timely visions. This chapter encourages believers to seek divine insight for their lives, document their spiritual visions, and act decisively to fulfill them, thereby making a significant impact in a world in desperate need of God's light.

CHAPTER 4

# HEAVENLY VISION THAT CONFRONTS THE GATES OF HELL

**Bible Verse**
"Whereupon, O king Agrippa, I was not disobedient unto the heavenly vision." - Acts 16:19 KJV

**Introduction**

This chapter delves into the transformative and empowering role of a heavenly vision in a believer's life, emphasizing the necessity of aligning with God's divine plan amidst spiritual and societal challenges.

**Word of Wisdom**

*"Myles Munroe defined vision as 'starting what God has already completed.' The Lord isn't trying to figure out what to do with your life. From the foundation of the world, He knew you inti-*

*mately, planned out your life, and perfectly designed and suited you for His plan."*
*Mark Cowart*

## Main Theme

The main theme of this chapter focuses on understanding and pursuing a God-given vision that has the power to confront and overcome spiritual darkness. It highlights the importance of divine guidance, spiritual discipline, and commitment to God's timing and will.

## Key Points

• Spiritual vision is essential for seeing and participating in God's work in the world.

• Writing down the vision helps ensure that it does not fade from memory and remains a guiding force.

• God has an individual plan for everyone, written before their creation.

• Believers must actively seek and follow the heavenly vision to avoid spiritual pitfalls.

• Understanding God's timing is crucial to fulfilling the vision He has provided.

• The power to fulfill God's vision comes from Him, not from human strength or ability.

SUMMARY OF THE POWER OF VISION

## Key Themes

- **The Power of Written Vision**: Writing down one's vision as revealed by God serves as a critical reminder and a physical representation of faith commitments. This practice not only preserves the vision during challenging times but also serves as a roadmap, guiding actions and decisions according to divine priorities.
- **The Role of Divine Timing in Vision Fulfillment**: Understanding and aligning with God's timing are essential for the realization of heavenly visions. This alignment ensures that believers are acting in concert with God's broader plan, maximizing the impact of their actions on the spiritual battlefield.
- **The Dangers of Spiritual Blindness**: Without spiritual vision, believers can fall prey to mundane desires and lose sight of their divine purpose. Spiritual blindness leads to a life devoid of the fullness and richness of God's plans, limiting believers' effectiveness in the kingdom.
- **The Impact of Vision on Spiritual Warfare**: A God-given vision equips believers to effectively confront and overcome the gates of hell. This vision provides not only the sight needed to perceive spiritual realities but also the strength and strategy to engage in spiritual battles.
- **The Importance of Spiritual Discipline and Development**: Pursuing a heavenly vision requires rigorous spiritual

discipline and continual development. Believers must cultivate their relationship with God through prayer, study, and obedience to ensure they are prepared to receive and act upon divine insights.

## Conclusion

"Heavenly Vision that Confronts the Gates of Hell" emphasizes the transformative impact of aligning one's life with a God-given vision. It challenges believers to actively seek and adhere to the divine blueprint for their lives, using the tools of writing, disciplined spiritual development, and a deep understanding of God's timing. Through this alignment, believers are equipped to shine as lights in the darkness, bringing glory to God and advancing His kingdom on earth.

## CHAPTER 5

# THE POWER OF RIGHT THINKING

**Bible Verse**

"For as he thinketh in his heart, so is he." — Proverbs 23:7

**Introduction**

This chapter explores the significant impact of imagination and right thinking on a believer's life, asserting that our thoughts and imaginations shape our reality and spiritual destiny. It emphasizes the spiritual and practical importance of guarding one's mind and aligning thoughts with God's Word.

**Word of Wisdom**

*"Whatever you allow in your mind can drop down into your spirit, and then it's basically on its way to coming to pass."*
*Mark Cowart*

## Main Theme

The main theme centers on the transformative power of imagination and right thinking, viewing them as spiritual warfare tools that either lead to life and fulfillment of God's purpose or to spiritual decay.

## Key Points

- Imagination is a gift from God and a powerful tool in spiritual warfare.

- Negative and positive imaginations have tangible effects on one's life.

- Right thinking aligns with biblical principles to foster spiritual and material prosperity.

- Spiritual vigilance over one's thoughts is essential to prevent negative spiritual outcomes.

- Thoughts are foundational to forming imaginations which can then manifest in reality.

- The media and culture significantly influence thoughts and imaginations, impacting society's moral fabric.

## Key Themes

- **Impact of Media on Imagination**: The media has a profound impact on shaping imaginations, often sowing seeds that can lead to either positive or negative societal outcomes. Believers must be particularly discerning about their media consumption,

as what is absorbed can deeply influence spiritual and mental states.
- **Guardianship of the Mind**: Proactively guarding one's thoughts is crucial in maintaining spiritual health and alignment with God's will. This includes not only monitoring what one consumes through media but also actively engaging with the Bible and positive influences to fortify the mind against spiritual attacks.
- **Creative Power of Thoughts**: Thoughts and imaginations are not merely passive reflections but active creators of our life's narrative. Understanding this creative power underscores the necessity of aligning one's thoughts with God's purposes and promises.
- **Subconscious Influence on Behavior**: Much of human behavior is influenced by the subconscious mind, which executes actions based on deeply ingrained beliefs and habits formed by repeated thoughts. This highlights the importance of regularly nurturing the mind with truth and life-affirming thoughts.
- **Spiritual and Practical Application of Imagination**: The application of imagination is not limited to spiritual aspects; it also extends to practical areas of life such as innovation, problem-solving, and personal development. Believers are encouraged to use their God-given imagination not only for personal growth but also for advancing the Kingdom of God.

## Conclusion

"The Power of Right Thinking" serves as a critical reminder of the biblical truth that our thoughts shape our lives. By cultivating a disciplined mind focused on God's truth, believers can harness their imagination to fulfill divine purposes, counteract negative cultural influences, and achieve a spiritually enriching and impactful life.

## CHAPTER 6

# THE ROLE OF TESTING IN THE POWER OF VISION

### Bible Verse

"Then Jesus, being filled with the Holy Spirit, returned from the Jordan and was led by the Spirit into the wilderness, being tempted for forty days by the devil." — Luke 4:1-2 NKJV

### Introduction

This chapter emphasizes the importance of testing in the development and realization of one's vision. It highlights how testing strengthens faith, prepares individuals for spiritual and natural promotion, and is an inevitable part of a life lived in accordance with God's purposes.

### Word of Wisdom

*"A faith that has not been tested cannot be trusted." Mark Cowart*

## Main Theme

Testing is integral to spiritual growth and the manifestation of one's vision. Through various forms of trials and temptations, a believer's faith is refined, proving essential for both spiritual maturity and fulfillment of God's divine purpose.

## Key Points

• Testing is inevitable and essential for growth in both natural and spiritual realms.

• Distinguishing between tests, trials, and temptations is crucial for spiritual understanding.

• Spiritual growth is impossible without the testing of faith.

• Tests can lead to spiritual promotion and greater responsibilities.

• Proper preparation can transform the perception and impact of tests.

• Jesus Christ's life exemplifies how one can successfully navigate divine tests.

## Key Themes

- **Purpose and Power of Testing**:
  Understanding the purpose behind tests and trials can shift one's perspective to embrace them rather than avoid them. Recognizing that testing refines and proves one's faith helps in cultivating

endurance and readiness for divine assignments.

- **Distinction Between Testing and Temptation**: It is vital to recognize the differences between testing, which strengthens and prepares us for God's promises, and temptations, which aim to lead us away from God's path. This discernment is key to responding correctly in various situations.
- **Preparation for Testing**: Being prepared for unexpected tests, much like being ready for a surprise exam, can reduce anxiety and increase confidence. Regular engagement with the Word of God equips believers with wisdom and knowledge to face any challenge.
- **Biblical Examples of Testing**: The life of Jesus Christ provides the ultimate blueprint for handling divine tests. His approach to trials, especially during His time in the wilderness and at Gethsemane, offers profound insights into the nature of obedience and submission to God's will.
- **Impact of Testing on Vision Fulfillment**: Tests not only prepare believers for personal growth but also ensure they are equipped to carry out the vision God has set for them. Successfully navigating tests can lead to spiritual promotions and new opportunities for ministry and influence.

## Conclusion

"The Role of Testing in the Power of Vision" underlines the critical role that trials play in a believer's life, marking them not as punishments but as opportunities for growth and confirmation of faith. By enduring and overcoming these tests, believers align more closely with God's purposes, advancing towards fulfilling their divine destiny while being transformed into His likeness.

CHAPTER 7

# KINGDOM DISCIPLES RUNNING WITH THE HEAVENLY VISION

### Bible Verse

"In Mark 12:29-30, Jesus said that the greatest, first, and most important commandment is to love the Lord your God with all your heart, with all your soul, with all your mind, and with all your strength. He said the second is likened to it—that you love your neighbor as yourself."

### Introduction

This chapter explores the deep connection between loving God and loving one's neighbor as foundational to embracing and running with a heavenly vision. It discusses how the infusion of divine love enables believers to overcome adversities and align with God's purposes.

### Word of Wisdom

*"You really can't love your neighbor*

*like you should without the love of God in your heart." Mark Cowart*

## Main Theme

The dual commandments of loving God and neighbor are not just moral imperatives but the engine that powers the believer's vision and mission in the Kingdom of God. This love is the force that propels disciples to live out their heavenly visions.

## Key Points

• Loving God with all one's heart is essential to understanding and fulfilling one's divine purpose.

• The ability to love others truly stems from the regeneration and renewal experienced through the Holy Spirit.

• Challenges and adversities are to be expected when pursuing a heavenly vision.

• Dreams and visions are integral to realizing God's plan for one's life.

• The enemy uses fear and distraction to deter believers from their divine path.

• The power of prayer and the guidance of the Holy Spirit are crucial in overcoming spiritual warfare related to dreams and visions.

## Key Themes

- **Divine Love as Foundation for Obedience**: True obedience to God's commandments requires a heart transformed by His love, which then naturally extends to loving others. This transformation is crucial for bearing the fruits of the Spirit and effectively ministering to others.
- **Importance of Dreams in Spiritual Guidance**: Dreams, whether they are divine night visions or conscious aspirations, play a critical role in shaping and directing the believer's journey. Understanding and discerning the source and purpose of dreams is essential for alignment with God's will.
- **Adversity as a Catalyst for Spiritual Growth**: Encountering opposition and hardship is part of pursuing a heavenly vision, but these challenges are opportunities for growth and affirmation of one's faith and commitment to God's plan.
- **Role of the Holy Spirit in Empowering Vision**: The Holy Spirit not only imbues believers with the ability to love God and neighbor but also empowers them to dream big and pursue those dreams despite opposition and fear instilled by the enemy.
- **Practical Steps to Cultivate and Realize Vision**: Engaging actively with one's dreams by writing them down, praying over them, and seeking God's

guidance through the Holy Spirit are practical steps that help in the realization of a heavenly vision.

## Conclusion

"Kingdom Disciples Running with the Heavenly Vision" emphasizes that the core of fulfilling God's vision for one's life lies in loving Him and others profoundly and genuinely. This love is the prerequisite for overcoming spiritual battles and advancing the Kingdom of God through one's life and actions. It calls for an active engagement with divine inspirations and a commitment to turning them into reality.

## CHAPTER 8

# AMERICA: A MODERN-DAY MANIFESTATION OF THE HEAVENLY VISION

### Bible Verse

"Proclaim Liberty Throughout All the Land Unto All the Inhabitants thereof" - Leviticus 25:10.

### Introduction

This chapter examines the United States as a nation founded on Christian principles and divine providence, arguing that its founding and continued existence are deeply entwined with a spiritual mission.

### Word of Wisdom

*"The only way that we won our fight for independence was by a firm reliance on the protection of Divine Providence."*
*Mark Cowart*

## Main Theme

The chapter portrays America as a unique example of a nation built under God's guidance, meant to uphold liberty and spread the gospel worldwide, even as it faces modern challenges that threaten its foundational principles.

## Key Points

• America's founding is deeply rooted in Christian principles and divine guidance.

• The liberties that define America are increasingly under threat in modern times.

• Founding fathers envisioned America as a beacon of freedom and righteousness.

• Current societal issues are seen as deviations from the nation's founding values.

• The historical significance of the U.S. is portrayed as a model for godly governance.

## Key Themes

- **Historical Foundations and Spiritual Mandate**: The United States was conceived with a clear divine purpose, intertwining its political and spiritual missions to act as a beacon of Christian values and liberty to the world.
- **Challenges to Foundational Liberties**: In recent years, the erosion of foundational American liberties highlights the need for

a recommitment to the principles that defined the nation's establishment.
- **Role of Divine Providence in America's Founding**: The miraculous success of America's fight for independence and subsequent rise to greatness is attributed to God's active involvement and favor, reflecting a divine plan for the nation.
- **Impact of Secular Influences on National Values**: The decline in societal adherence to Christian values is presented as a threat to the nation's stability and divine mission, urging a return to religious commitment.
- **The Power of Vision in Overcoming Adversity**: By embracing the original vision for the nation, rooted in faith and divine guidance, Americans can confront and overcome the challenges posed by modern secularism and moral decline.

## Conclusion

The chapter concludes with a call to Americans to rediscover and recommit to the heavenly vision upon which the nation was founded. It stresses the importance of upholding the Christian principles of the founding fathers to navigate contemporary challenges and ensure the nation fulfills its divine purpose. This recommitment is essential not only for America's prosperity but for its role as a global spiritual leader.

Harrison House is a Spirit-filled, Word of Faith Christian publisher dedicated to spreading the message of faith, hope, and love through our wide range of inspiring publications. Committed to the messages that highlight the power of the Word and Spirit, we provide books, devotionals, and study guides that empower believers to live victorious, faith-filled lives.

Our resources are designed to help readers grow spiritually, strengthen their faith, and experience the transformative power of God's Word. Harrison House is passionate about equipping Christians with the tools they need to fulfill their divine purpose and impact the world for Christ.

www.ingramcontent.com/pod-product-compliance
Lightning Source LLC
LaVergne TN
LVHW051513070426
835507LV00022B/3086